JANE AUSTEN

JANE AUSTEN

by

LORD DAVID CECIL

THE LESLIE STEPHEN LECTURE DELIVERED
BEFORE THE UNIVERSITY OF CAMBRIDGE
ON I MAY 1935

CAMBRIDGE
AT THE UNIVERSITY PRESS
1935

CAMBRIDGE
UNIVERSITY PRESS

University Printing House, Cambridge CB2 8BS, United Kingdom

Published in the United States of America by Cambridge University Press, New York

Cambridge University Press is part of the University of Cambridge.

It furthers the University's mission by disseminating knowledge in the pursuit of education, learning and research at the highest international levels of excellence.

www.cambridge.org
Information on this title: www.cambridge.org/9781107635418

© Cambridge University Press 1935

First edition April 1935
Reprinted October 1935
First published 1935
First paperback edition 2014

A catalogue record for this publication is available from the British Library

ISBN 978-1-107-63541-8 Paperback

JANE AUSTEN

I cannot begin without acknowledging how
deeply I feel the honour of addressing you to-
day. It is not so many years since I first visited
Cambridge as a humble undergraduate from
Oxford. That I should now be chosen to de-
liver an official lecture to the University and in
the name of so honourable a Foundation fills
me with a pride, a pleasure and a wonder that
might well stifle my voice and tie my tongue.
But I am kept in countenance by the conscious-
ness that I am not alone—that any wonder I
may feel would have been shared by the author
who is my subject. If I am surprised to find myself lecturing to you, Jane Austen would have
been still more surprised to find herself being
lectured about. For—it is the most striking fact
discovered by her life history—she did not take
her work very seriously.

Hers was no career of solemn and solitary
self-dedication. Neat, elegant and sociable, she

spent most of her day sitting in the drawing-room of the parsonage which was her home, sewing and gossiping. From time to time, it is said, she would begin to laugh, and then, stepping across to the writing-table, she would scribble a few lines on a sheet of paper. But if visitors called she slipt the pages under the blotter; when the pages had accumulated into a story, she let it lie for years in a drawer unread. And when at last it did emerge to the public gaze, she refused in the slightest degree to modify the conventional order of her life to suit with the character of a professional author-ess. As for the applause of posterity, she seems never to have given it a moment's thought: it was no part of her sensible philosophy to worry about admiration that she would not live to enjoy.

Yet one hundred and nineteen years have passed since her death, and yearly the applause of posterity has grown louder. There are those who do not like her; as there are those who do not like sunshine or unselfishness. But the very nervous defiance with which they shout their dissatisfaction shows that they know they are a despised minority. All discriminating critics admire her books, most educated readers enjoy them; her fame, if not highest among English novelists, is of all the most secure.

These are interesting facts. But they are not really surprising. Success in the art of letters is not so exclusively the affair of tension and temperament that some people seem to fancy. It is, strangely enough, an affair of art. The most successful writer is he who obeys most strictly the laws which govern the art of his choice. And of all those who have chosen the novel none has been more careful to keep its laws than Jane Austen. It is this that gives her her advantage over other English novelists. She was not the most talented, she did not write about the most sensational topics; but as a master of her craft she outshines them all. And when we turn to analyse our admiration for her it is the triumphs of her craft that first strike us.

To begin with we notice that she obeys the first rule of all imaginative composition, that she stays within the range of her imaginative inspiration. A work of art is born of the union of the artist's experience and his imagination. But only certain aspects of his experience stir a deep enough response in his personality to generate his imaginative spark: only when it is inspired by them does his work have artistic life. It is his first obligation therefore to choose themes within the range of this experience. Now Jane Austen's imaginative range was in some respects a very limited one. It was, in the first place, confined to human beings in their personal relations. Man in relation to God, to politics, to abstract ideas, passed her by: it was only when she saw him with his family and his neighbours that her creative impulse began to stir to activity. She sees Mrs Brown not as a soul or as a citizen but only as the wife of Mr Brown. Her view was further limited by the fact that in general she looked at Mrs Brown in one perspective, the satiric. Jane Austen was a comedian. Her first literary impulse was humorous; and to the end of her life humour was an integral part of her creative process: as her imagination starts to function a smile begins to spread itself across her features. And the smile is the signature on the finished work. It is the angle of her satiric vision, the light of her wit that gives its peculiar glitter and proportion to her picture of the world.

All this meant that she could only be successful with themes that turned on personal relationships and were susceptible in some degree of satiric treatment. Jane Austen, it is her triumph, realised this. She was once asked—and by no less a person than the librarian of the Prince Regent—to write a historical novel about the fortunes of the House of Coburg. But she refused this majestic proposal on the ground that it would be unwise for her to leave her "small square, two inches, of ivory". And, except in a few minor episodes, she never did leave it. All her stories turn on personal relationships, between friends, between parents and

children, between men and women in love—
and they turn on nothing else at all. She was
equally careful to choose themes with satirical
implications. She lived through the French
Revolution and the Napoleonic Wars, but no
shadow of their storm is permitted to confuse
the firm bright clarity of her vision. There are
no adventures in her books, no abstract ideas,
no romantic reveries, no death scenes. Nor
does she give much space to the impressions of
the senses. This was from no incapacity on her
part. The delicate glimpses of landscape that
make soft the background of *Persuasion*, the
squalid interior of Captain Price's home at
Portsmouth where Fanny's eyes "could only
wander from the walls marked by her father's
head to...the tea-board never thoroughly
clean, the cups and saucers wiped in streaks, the
milk a mixture of motes floating in thin blue",
show that she could paint for the eye with perfect certainty if she had wanted. But satire, like
Blake's tear, is an intellectual thing, a critical
comment on life. And the impressions of the

senses are conveyed not by critical comment but by direct record. To interpolate many such records into a comedy will disperse its comic atmosphere. Jane Austen avoided them.

She avoided jarring characters too. Two-thirds of her dramatis personae are regular comic character-parts like Mr Collins or Mrs Allen. And even those figures with whom she is most in sympathy, even her heroines, are almost all touched with the comic spirit. Two of them, Emma and Elizabeth Bennet, are a great deal cleverer than most heroines of fiction; one of them, Anne Elliot, is very good. But all three are flesh and blood work-a-day creatures, able to laugh, if not to be laughed at. Only once, in *Mansfield Park*, did Jane Austen try another type; and she failed. The main lines of Fanny Price's character are admirably con-ceived, and treasures of subtle observation are poured out on her. But the innocent romantic sweetness, the lovely youthful austerity, which should have been her charm, cannot be con-veyed in a comedy vein. So that when she comes to describe them Jane Austen's hand for once falters. Fanny is a little wooden, a little charmless, and rather a prig.

Indeed youthful romance, unless she could laugh at it, was not within Jane Austen's province. The nature of her talent imposed a third limitation on her; it made her unable to express impulsive emotion directly. She surveyed her creatures with too detached an irony for her to identify herself with them sufficiently to voice their unthinking gushes of feeling. On the few occasions she tried she becomes self-conscious, unreal and, incredible to relate, rather absurd. "The evergreen," exclaims Fanny, rhapsodising in a Wordsworthian moment over the Mansfield plantations, "how beautiful, how welcome, how wonderful the evergreen." But such lapses are rare. Generally Jane Austen is as artful in avoiding the occasion for them as in everything else. She traces brilliantly the effect of emotion, the way it heats a situation, modifies character; but she expresses it only by implication. Her plots turn on love, but only one of her lovers, the self-controlled Mr Knightley, do we hear declare his passion. We are shown exactly how Anne Elliot's love of nature coloured her mood, but she is never allowed to tell us of it in person.

Jane Austen's natural range was further bounded by the limitations imposed by circumstances. No author, except a fantasist, can make anything living of worlds of which he is not personally experienced. The world of Jane Austen's experience was a very small one. She was a woman in an age when women were forbidden by convention from moving in any society except that in which they were born: and the class she was born in, that of the smaller English gentry, was the one most enslaved to convention. But she kept to it. Her stories all take place in England, all in one class. Further, she is one of the few women novelists who have accepted the limitations of their sex. She never describes a scene in which no woman is present; her heroes are shown to us, fragmentarily, and with character and motives in part unexplained, as they appeared to the girls with whom they came in contact. Here as elsewhere she is true almost uniformly to the first rule of literary art, she excludes from her books all aspects of life that cannot pass through the crucible of her imagination. So that every inch of her book is vital.

She is not only true to the rules of literary art in general; she is also true to the particular laws that govern the art of the novel. The novelist has a more complex task than the poet. For he sets out to give a picture of the world as it is. And this confronts him with two problems. First he has to reconcile reality with imagination. Like all works of art his book should be an expression of his personality; but it must also be a convincing record of facts. And he can only attain the highest success if he satisfies both these conditions equally. Many great novelists do not. *Jane Eyre* is drenched through with the lurid element of Charlotte Brontë's imagination; but as a picture of a governess's life in the 1840's it is, to say the least of it, unconvincing. Trollope on the other hand tends to present us with a mere accurate photograph untinged by the colour of an individual vision. Now Jane Austen's imagination was, as we have seen, a comedian's imagination. Her problem is to draw a true picture of life which should also amuse us. And in the masterpieces of her maturity, in *Emma* and *Persuasion*, she succeeds perfectly. She paints the surface of English life with a meticulous and Dutch accuracy; Miss Bates is a bore exactly like a hundred bores we fly from every day. Only— we find ourselves hanging on her words; by a delightful miracle she has been made entertaining. Jane Austen could perform similar miracles upon even less promising material. Examine the account in *Emma* of how the news of Mrs Churchill's death was received at Highbury. "It was felt as such things must be felt. Everybody had a degree of gravity and sorrow; tenderness towards the departed, solicitude for the surviving friends; and, in a reasonable time, curiosity to know where she would be buried.

Goldsmith tells us that when lovely woman stoops to folly, she has nothing to do but to die; and when she stoops to be disagreeable, it is equally to be recommended as a clearer of ill fame. Mrs Churchill, after being disliked at least twenty-five years, was now spoken of with compassionate allowances. In one point she was fully justified. She had never been admitted before to be seriously ill. The event acquitted her of all the fancifulness and all the selfishness of imaginary complaints." Here is no comic distortion of sad reality. This, we know, is exactly how the news of such a death would be received by such people. Yet we cannot read it without laughing.

Even when Jane Austen is not out primarily to make us laugh she never wholly leaves the realm of comedy. She describes Anne's love for Wentworth with an exquisite sympathy; but her sympathy does not blind her to whatever ironical implications it may have. Anne is sure that when Lady Russell looks out of the carriage, in which they are driving, it is to gaze at Wentworth. Jane Austen notes with amusement that in reality it is to see what is in the shops. However intractable her material may seem to be, she manages to tinge it with a comic tone.

It is partly due to the judgment with which she chooses her angle of vision. She puts herself in a position in which the humorous aspects of her subject stand out most obviously, so that by only setting out the facts in their unemphasised sobriety she can make them amusing. Mrs Churchill's death had no doubt its solemn aspects, but they were not noticeable from the point of view from which Jane Austen looks at it. Comedy is also implicit in the manner in which she tells her story. Her irony, her delicate ruthless irony, is of the very substance of her style. It never obtrudes itself; sometimes it only glints out in a turn of phrase. But it is never absent for more than a paragraph; and her most straightforward piece of exposition is tart with its perfume. Mrs Bennet "was a woman of mean understanding, little information, and uncertain temper. When she was discontented she fancied herself nervous. The business of her life was to get her daughters married; its solace was visiting and news". From a serious point of view this is an admirable summary of Mrs Bennet's character. Tolstoy himself could not have stated it more completely. But Tolstoy would have stated it without a smile; while every word of Jane Austen's, every curt rhythm, every neat antithesis betrays she is not speaking with a straight face. By the mere tone of her voice she sets drab reality dancing and sparkling with the sunlight of her comic vision.

Her troubles are not over when she has satisfied the rival claims of fact and imagination. Here we come to the second problem with which the nature of his material confronts the novelist. A work of art is an orderly unity; life is a heterogeneous tangle. The writer has to devise a form for his inspiration which will at once please us as an artistic pattern and give us a convincing impression of disorderly reality.

In addition to reconciling fact and imagination he must reconcile fact and form. It is a hard task: and, it cannot be said that Jane Austen always succeeded in it. In *Northanger Abbey* and *Sense and Sensibility* she sacrifices fact to form. The character of Edward Ferrars, the eccentric conduct of General Tilney, these are too palpably pieces of machinery invented to fit the exigencies of the plot. In *Mansfield Park* she sacrifices form to fact. The original design of the book obviously intended Henry Crawford to fill the rôle of villain. But as she works Jane Austen's creative power gets out of control, Henry Crawford comes to life as a sympathetic character; and under the pressure of his personality the plot takes a turn, of which the only logical conclusion is his marriage with the heroine, Fanny. Jane Austen was not one to be put upon by her creatures in this way. In the last three chapters she violently wrenches the story back into its original course: but only at the cost of making Henry act in a manner wholly inconsistent with the rest of his character.

At her best, however, she keeps the balance between fact and form as no other English novelist has ever done. She neither twists reality to fit a logical scheme like Henry James, nor like Scott lets life tumble pell-mell about the reader's head in indeterminate confusion. Her stories are meticulously integrated; not a character, not an episode but makes its necessary contribution to the development of the plot. Only, we do not notice it. The scaffolding is so artfully overlaid with the foliage of her invention that it seems a free growth. She makes her incidents so natural, endows her characters with so independent a reality, that it is possible to read about them without ever realising that they are part of a scheme at all. Even if we do realise it we are half in doubt as to whether it is an intentional scheme. The picture she presents to us seems no calculated composition but rather a glimpse of life itself; life caught at a moment when its shifting elements have chanced to group themselves into a temporary symmetry. *Emma* and *Pride and Prejudice* are as logically constructed as a detective story; yet they give us all the sense of spontaneous life we get from a play of Chekhov.

Persuasion is less impeccably designed: Mrs Smith, like Edward Ferrars, is a bit of lifeless machinery. But it is its author's greatest formal achievement. For in it she gives her story not only a dramatic but also a spiritual unity. Its subject is love, the constant love renounced from an unwise prudence, that Anne Elliot feels for Wentworth. And every episode of the story refers to this subject. The rash happy marriage of the Crofts, the love, enduring through hardship, of the Harvilles, the inconstancy of Benwick and Louisa Musgrove—all these, by contrast or similarity, illustrate Anne's situation: now in the major key, now in the minor, now simply, now with variations, they repeat the main theme of the symphony. Even the tender autumnal weather in which most of the action takes place echoes and symbolises the prevailing mood of the story. Such singleness of structure gives *Persuasion* an emotional concentration unattainable by any other means. Yet this structure is not emphasised in such a way as to destroy the illusion of every-day reality. The reader never feels that Benwick and the rest of them are put in to play their part in the harmony, but just because they happened to be features of the bit of actual life Jane Austen has chosen to describe. By a supreme feat of dexterity she has managed to compose a symphony on the theme of love, which is also a realistic story of ordinary human beings.

Jane Austen then is the only English novelist who has managed fully to satisfy the three essential requirements of her art, the only one who has solved all three of its major problems. Certainly there is no reason to wonder at her reputation. And yet one cannot help feeling that something more is needed to account for it. Mere technical accomplishment is not enough to explain the impression she makes on us. After all, a work of art may be perfect technically and yet be a minor work, a porcelain vase, an ormolu snuff-box. And Jane

Austen, though she is not one of the imperial monarchs of fiction, is still less a manufacturer of snuff-boxes. The absorbing, searching interest she awakes in the mind—so that one turns to her again and again and always finds something new to think about—is one only stirred by works of major art. Her books—it is the second reason for their enduring popularity—have a universal significance.

This is due in the first place to the sheer strength of their author's talent; to the fact that she is endowed in the highest degree with the one essential gift of the novelist, the power to create living characters. It is true that she only draws them in their private aspect. But this is not a superficial aspect. A man's relation to his wife and children is at least as important a part of his life as his relation to his beliefs and career; and reveals him as fundamentally. Indeed it reveals his moral side more fundamentally. If you want to know about a man's talents you should see him in society, if you want to know about his temper you should see him at home.

Nor is Jane Austen's view rendered less fundamental by the fact that she shows him as a rule not in moments of crisis but in the trivial incidents of every day. Life is made up of little things, and human nature reveals itself in them as fully as in big ones: a picnic shows up selfishness, kindness, vanity, sincerity, as much as a battle. Only you must have the faculty to discern them. Jane Austen had. Her eye for the surface of personality is unerring. Not Dickens himself can visualise outward idiosyncrasies of his creatures more vividly, their manner, their charm, their tricks of speech.

But unlike Dickens, Jane Austen also realises the psychological organism that underlies speech and manner. She is not content just to dash down her intuitive impressions of people; her lucid knife-edged mind was always at work penetrating beneath such impressions to discern their cause, discover the principles of her subject's conduct, the peculiar combination of qualities that go to make up his individuality. And she shows us surface peculiarities always in relation to these essentials. The consequence is she does not need to present man involved in major catastrophes. If for once her plot does entail her portraying her characters in moments of serious crisis, she can do it perfectly. Louisa Musgrove, skipping down the steps of the Cobb at Lyme, trips and falls apparently lifeless. With acute insight Jane Austen illustrates the way the rest of the party react to this disaster: how the egotistic Mary Musgrove is absorbed in her egotistic agitation, how the unrestrained Henrietta collapses, how Wentworth's sympathetic imagination conjures up at once the effect of the news on Louisa's parents, how Anne alone, unselfish, self-controlled Anne, keeps her head. But though we admire Jane Austen's insight it tells us nothing new about these people; the uneventful walks and dinner parties where we have already seen them have revealed their disposition so fully that we could have foretold how they would behave.

Indeed Jane Austen's understanding of the moral nature of man is, within the limitations of her experience, complete. She may not have known all that the people of her world thought and fancied, but she knew exactly which was good and which bad, discriminated exactly the individual shade of their goodness or badness, exactly perceived how it showed itself in their behaviour. Nothing escapes her, nothing baffles her, nothing deceives her. However slight its manifestation, however muffled by convention or disguised by personal charm, unfailingly she detects the essential quality of character. The Miss Bertrams "joined to beauty and brilliant acquirements a manner naturally easy, and carefully formed to general civility and obligingness,... Their vanity was in such good order, that they seemed to be quite free from it, and gave themselves no airs; while the praises attending such behaviour,... served to strengthen them in believing they had no faults". Only two sentences: but they make us understand the Miss Bertrams completely.

Such penetration enabled her to elucidate far

more complex characters than most novelists. The young ladies who play the chief rôles in her stories are more intricately conceived than those of any English novelist before George Eliot. Emma is a complex mixture of vanity, wilfulness, and fundamental generous feeling; Mary Crawford a complex mixture of sympathy and selfishness, shallowness and common-sense. Each of these qualities is precisely defined for us. Yet the result is no impersonal analysed psychological case like those which make dreary the stories of some of our distinguished contemporaries. The vivid intensity of Jane Austen's vision fuses them together into a single breathing moving human being. Emma and Mary Crawford are equally real as personalities and as characters.

Not less acute is Jane Austen's insight into the processes of the heart: the minute symptoms—half-said word, instinctive imperceptible movement—by which people betray an emotion. We *know* that Darcy is still in love with Elizabeth though he has not spoken to her all the evening because "he brought back his coffee cup himself" to the table where she was pouring out: we realise Anne's complete absorption in Wentworth as we watch her move almost involuntarily to the table at which he has been writing the moment he has left the room. And Jane Austen can follow through its most hidden and discursive windings the course by which feeling expresses itself in the mind. Fanny Price, agonised with jealousy, is kept waiting for her ride while Edmund is taking her rival for a turn on her horse. She does not admit she is jealous even to herself, but her irritation vents itself in a sudden spirt of indignation at the inconsiderate way they are tiring the animal. "She began to think it rather hard upon the mare to have such double duty; if she were forgotten, the poor mare should be remembered."

This quotation illustrates another of Jane Austen's particular merits, her impartiality. It is the most important consequence of her consistently ironical attitude that she never idealises.

Her most virtuous characters have their faults. And, what is more striking, she shows us how these faults are integral to their natures. Fanny is unselfish and high-minded. But Jane Austen perceives that these same virtues bring along with them, as a necessary corollary, certain weaknesses; that Fanny's very habit of self-abnegation led her, if for once she had a selfish feeling, to disguise it from herself; that her very strictness of principle was liable to make her unjust to her more frivolous rival.

Jane Austen is equally honest about the characters she did not like. She loathed Mrs Norris —who could do otherwise?—and thought her far more odious than harmless silly Mrs Price. But she sees that the same meddling energy which made her so disagreeable would have fitted her far better than Mrs Price to cope with the difficulties of a poor sailor's wife with a large family. And she says so. This impartiality gives her characters volume: they are not brilliantly drawn silhouettes, but solid, three-dimensional figures, who can be looked at from several sides.

And there is a huge number of them. Jane Austen's range of character is very large. She painted on such a narrow canvas that people have not always realised this. But a wide canvas does not necessarily mean a wide range. Thackeray painted on a vast one, but his range of characters is small. For he always repeats them; his good women are all pictures of the same person in a different dress. Jane Austen's good women, Anne Elliot, Elinor Dashwood, Fanny Price, are all different. In her six books she never repeats a single character. The snobbishness of the Rev. Mr Collins is unlike that of the Rev. Mr Elton: Isabella Thorpe and Lucy Steele are both calculating flirts but not the same sort of calculating flirt: there is all the difference in the world between the vulgarity of Mrs Bennet and the vulgarity of Mrs Jennings. Out of her small parsonage house Jane Austen's gay wand conjures innumerable troops of unique individuals.

So comprehensive and so searching a view of human nature inevitably invests her achievement with a universal character. For all that she paints the nineteenth-century English scene with so sedulous an accuracy, this accuracy is an unimportant part of the impression that she makes. *Mansfield Park* does not, like *Cranford* appeal to us first of all by its period charm: we do not remember Mr Elton as we remember Archdeacon Grantly because he is such a true picture of an English clergyman. He could turn into a Scotch minister and we should still recognise him. For he lives not in virtue of his likeness to national character but to essential human nature. Essential human nature—this is always Jane Austen's preoccupation. Her characters are universal types. Miss Bates is the type of all bores, Mrs Elton the type of all pushing vulgarians, Marianne Dashwood the type of all undisciplined romantics; when Mr Woodhouse tells us that his grandchildren are "all remarkably clever...they will come and stand by my chair and say 'grandpapa can you give me a bit of string?'" he sums up the fatuous fondness of all grandparents; when Mr Darcy says "I have been selfish all my life in practice but not in principle" he confesses the weakness of high-minded dominating males in every age and climate. Jane Austen's realistic English drawing-rooms, like the unfurnished ante-chambers of French classical drama, are theatres in which elemental human folly and inconsistency play out their eternal comedy.

This brings me to the second fact about her work which gives it a universal character. Like all great comedians, she satirises in relation to a universal standard of values: her books express a general view of life. It is the view of that eighteenth-century civilisation of which she was the last exquisite blossom. One might call it the moral-realistic view. Jane Austen was profoundly moral. She thought you lived only to be good, that it was the first duty of everyone to be sincere, unselfish and disinterested. But the very seriousness with which she held this conviction made her think it imperative to see life realistically. Good notions were to be acted upon; therefore you could only be sure they were good if they had passed the test of commonsense and experience. She despised all ideals, however lofty, that were not practical, all emotions, however soul-stirring, if they did not in fact make for the benefit and happiness of mankind. Indeed she did not value emotions as such at all. She reserved some of her most mischievous mockery for extravagant maternal affection and sentimental rhapsodising over nature. Love itself, though she understood its workings admirably, did not rouse her enthusiasm unless it was justified by reason, disciplined by self-control. She had little sympathy for romantic imprudence or credulous good nature; she was impatient of people with hearts of gold and heads of wood. And though she was not a slave to worldly considerations she thought it a mistake to overlook them entirely. It was wrong to marry for money, but it was silly to marry without it. Nor should one lightly break with convention. Only fools imagined they could live happily in the world without paying attention to what its inhabitants thought.

Further, her realism made her think it foolish to worry about evils one could not prevent. Life was clearly an imperfect affair at the best; but it had to be lived. And a sensible man, except in so far as it interfered with the performance of his duty, concentrated on life's pleasant aspects. "How horrible it is", she writes about a battle in the Peninsular War, "to have so many killed, and what a blessing that one cares for none of them." This robust attitude to the ills inevitable to mortality, is rare to-day—which is a pity. It is the only one in which a man of principle can live through troubled times without growing intolerably depressed.

This rational sense of the value of happiness is the origin of her third standard of judgment —taste. As much an artist in life as in her work, Jane Austen recognised that how you live is only second in importance to what you live for, that life is a question of form as well as of content. To be completely satisfactory as a human being you need to be not only good and sensible but also well-mannered and cultivated.

For intelligence and refinement add to the pleasantness of life. She did not admire noble savages or rough diamonds or genial slovenly vulgarians. If you could not manage to be good there was some merit in being good-mannered. Mansfield Park was not morally superior to Fanny's Portsmouth home, but it was preferable for "its elegance, propriety, regularity and harmony". It is this sensibility to the value of form which makes Jane Austen's view of life so much more convincing than those of the Victorians who followed her. There is nothing puritanical or provincial about it, it recognises that body and mind have their claims as well as soul, it is a civilised philosophy for civilised people.

And it permeates every aspect of her work. Not that she is a deliberate preacher using the novel as a means to teach her gospel. In a sense she was too confident in its truth. What was the point, she felt, in expounding principles which must be obvious to any rational person. Besides the spectacle of human ineptitude amused her too much for her to have any great wish to put an end to it. She wrote primarily just to entertain. But her view of life was so fundamental to her personality that her every imaginative conception is related to it. Not one of her characters, however farcical or however delightful, but is brought to trial before the triple bar of taste, sense and virtue; and if they fail to give satisfaction on any one of these counts, smiling but relentless she passes sentence on them. Her sense of justice is exquisite and implacable; neither pity nor anger can make it swerve from its course; she is never vindictive and never sentimental; she makes no exceptions in deference to public opinion or to her personal feelings. Mary Crawford is extremely sensible and as charming as Elizabeth Bennet herself. But she cannot face marrying a clergyman: she is condemned. Marianne Dashwood had no such worldly weakness; and she also is charming. But she is the prey of romantic illusions; and for this she too receives her punishment.

Jane Austen applies the standards of taste equally ruthlessly. Miss Bates was a bore but she was also a kind old spinster with an excellent heart. If Dickens had described her, her heart would have shed a softening halo over her boringness. Jane Austen does every justice to her good qualities; but she makes her as boring as she possibly can. Not grief itself can shield a character from the death-ray of her fastidiousness. "Mrs Musgrove was of a comfortable, substantial size, infinitely more fitted by nature to express good cheer and good humour than tenderness and sentiment;...Captain Wentworth should be allowed some credit for the self-command with which he attended to her large, fat sighings over the destiny of a son whom alive nobody had cared for. Personal size and mental sorrow have certainly no necessary proportions. A large bulky figure has as good a right to be in deep affliction as the most graceful set of limbs in the world. But, fair or not fair, there are unbecoming conjunctions, which reason will patronise in vain—

which taste cannot tolerate—which ridicule will seize." Jane Austen is not heartless, she sympathises fully with whatever is genuine in Mrs Musgrove's sorrow; but she sees there is something absurd about her even in lamentation. And she points it out.

Her outlook expresses itself as much in general structure as in detail. Her stories are not just strings of incident and character knit together by a plot for the sake of convenience. Each is built round a theme; and this theme illustrates some aspect of her view of life. They divided themselves into three groups. *Northanger Abbey* and *Sense and Sensibility* satirise that romantic philosophy which was sweeping the world in the early nineteenth century. Romanticism, referring all its judgments as it did to the guidance of the instinctive movements of heart and imagination, was profoundly alien to Jane Austen. In *Northanger Abbey* she laughs at its superficial aspects. Catherine Morland is a simple girl who is always making a fool of herself because she expects life to be like the romantic novels which are her favourite reading. *Sense and Sensibility* is a more fundamental attack. Elinor Dashwood guides her conduct by reason, Marianne by the impulses of her enthusiastic nature: the story shows how experience proves Elinor right and Marianne wrong. *Emma* and *Pride and Prejudice* deal with more personal questions. *Pride and Prejudice* exhibits the folly of trusting to first impressions uncorrected by mature observation. Elizabeth Bennet is misled by the immediate agreeability of the one and the haughty formality of the other, into liking Wickham and disliking Darcy: the action describes how further knowledge teaches her to reverse these opinions. *Emma*, Jane Austen's profoundest comedy, satirises the self-deceptions of vanity. Emma is a clever woman whose confidence in her own cleverness blinds her to reality. She spends her life in trying to re-arrange the lives of others; but her plans when put into practice only reveal her failure to understand either the dispositions of the people she is dealing with, or the true nature of her own feelings and motives. *Mansfield Park* and *Persuasion* are more serious. Though they are composed within the limitations of Jane Austen's comic convention, their subjects are not so essentially satirical. *Mansfield Park* contrasts worldliness with unworldliness; the story illustrates the superiority of the disinterested Fanny and Edmund to the crude worldly Bertrams on the one hand, and on the other hand, more subtly, to the clever worldly Crawfords. *Persuasion* is about love. How far should love be restrained by prudential considerations? It is a different sort of subject from that of her other books; and the pensive sympathy, with which she discusses it, betrays a softening of her prevailing mood. Sad experience has taught her that the problems of the heart are too momentous to be decided with the unhesitating confidence of her high-spirited youth. But the standard by which she decides them remains the same. Anne is declared mistaken in her early renunciation of Wentworth, not because love should override all other considerations, but because Wentworth was virtuous and industrious enough for a reasonable woman to risk poverty with him.

This considered intellectual foundation means that the interest of Jane Austen's books is far more serious than their surface appearance would lead us to expect. These spinsters and curates have the universal significance of the scheme of values in whose light they are presented to us: these quiet comedies of country life propound fundamental problems of human conduct. In every age, every country, people must decide whether they will direct their lives by feeling or reason, decide how much importance they should attach to considerations of prudence or worldly advantage; in every age and country, people are misled by first impressions, deceived by over-confidence in their own powers. The issues between Elinor and Marianne are the issues between Rousseau and Dr Johnson: the errors that are the undoing of Emma have undone many statesmen and social reformers; though the setting and costumes of

Mansfield Park may be those of *Cranford*, its drama expresses a criticism of life as comprehensive as that of *Madame Bovary*.

Nor does the limited theatre of its presentation impair the power of this criticism. On the contrary, it increases it. It gives it charm. The unique irresistible flavour of her work, its gay astringent buoyancy, its silvery commonsense arises from the unexpected combination of her realistic moralism with the polished serenity of its setting. Moreover the fact that she kept so carefully to the only world she knew thoroughly well, meant that she was not distracted by superficial idiosyncrasies, but could penetrate beneath them to perceive its more general significance. *Emma* is universal just because it is narrow; because it confines itself to the range of Jane Austen's profoundest vision.

For it is a profound vision. There are other views of life both higher and wider; concerned as it is exclusively with personal relationships, it leaves out several of the most important aspects of experience. But on her own ground

Jane Austen gets to the heart of the matter; her graceful unpretentious philosophy, founded as it is on an unwavering recognition of fact, directed by an unerring perception of moral quality, is as impressive as those of the most majestic novelists. Myself I find it more impressive. If I were in doubt as to the wisdom of one of my actions I should not consult Flaubert or Dostoievsky. The opinion of Balzac or Dickens would carry little weight with me: were Stendhal to rebuke me, it would only convince me I had done right: even in the judgment of Tolstoy I should not put complete confidence. But I should be seriously upset, I should worry for weeks and weeks, if I incurred the disapproval of Jane Austen.